SUPER CUTE

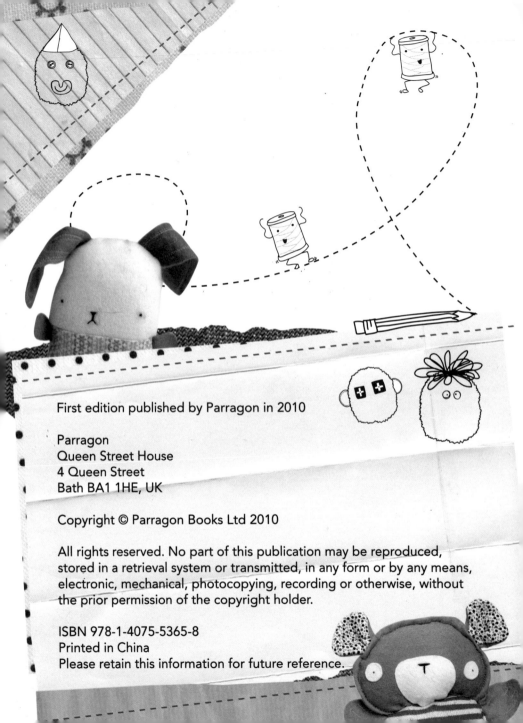

First edition published by Parragon in 2010

Parragon
Queen Street House
4 Queen Street
Bath BA1 1HE, UK

ISBN 978-1-4075-5365-8
Printed in China
Please retain this information for future reference.

SUPER CUTE

PaRragon

Bath · New York · Singapore · Hong Kong · Cologne · Delhi · Melbourne

Contents

Check out the very back of this book for some super-cute templates!

About this book

Do you love all things
SUPER CUTE and **CUDDLY?**

How would you like to make some yourself?
Take the makes in this book and let your
imagination run wild.

Feel free, inspired and creative.

HELLO

There are NO limits

The crafts and instructions are specific enough to help out a beginner, but they've got enough variety to please the pickiest of pros. Whatever your level, this book gives you the skills and guidance you need to make your own cuddly things.

The best part about the makes is that they're totally eco friendly and low cost. All you have to do is reduce, reuse and recycle — and raid your cupboards! Use clothes you've grown out of, stray buttons, ratty blankets, even old curtains.

JUST DON'T FORGET TO ASK YOUR PARENTS FIRST!

You've got everything you need here — an intro to sewing skills, some cool crafts with instructions, some templates and materials, suggestions on where to find fabric and accessories — so go for it: make something.......

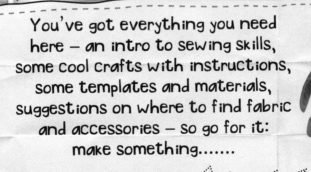

SUPER CUTE

7

Hello!

INSIDE THIS PACK

Tools & Techniques

9

IN YOUR SEWING KIT

You really don't need too many materials to get started. This book comes with some of them, and the rest you can find at sewing shops or even around your house.

Every sewing kit should have:

Needles
A mix of needles is best. Use medium-length, sharp needles for general sewing, and shorter quilting needles for the really finicky work. Needles with long eyes (the hole the thread goes through) are for embroidery.

Sewing thread
A whole load of different colours is a must for the modern sewer. You normally want to match the colour of the thread to the fabric, but sometimes you want it to stand out, so pick boring colours, such as black and white, and have vibrant colours like purple, too.

Embroidery thread
Embroidery thread is much thicker than sewing thread and is used to decorate rather than stitch fabric together.

Pins

You'll need pins to hold fabric in place while you lay it out and start sewing. Store your pins in a cool pincushion like the one on page 94.

Scissors

Use a small pair of scissors for cutting curves and clipping thread, and a large pair for cutting big pieces of fabric and big shapes. Check with an adult about these.

Ruler

For measuring lengths of your materials.

Glue

It's best to find some craft glue that you know will work on different types of fabric.

GLUE

Buttons

Never throw a stray button away! You never know when a lonely little button will be the perfect finishing touch to your make. Keep your buttons in a cool container.

Ribbon

Don't get rid of any ribbon either! Keep a collection of it — short pieces, long spools of it... and then you'll always have a way to glam up your makes.

11

FABRICS

When you're sewing, remember that every fabric is different.

FELT

Felt is the easiest material to handle. Even if you're just starting out, you (yes, you!) can handle it. Felt is easy to cut and it doesn't fray. The best kind of felt is an all-wool felt, although a kids' craft felt will work too. Remember that felt doesn't like to be bathed and might act up if you try to put it in water!

COTTON

If you're going to use cotton (like an old shirt), wash it first. That way it won't shrink if you wash it after you make it into something new, and your new item will smell nice and fresh (and not like an old shirt)!

FLEECE

An old fleece is a great material for making a blanket, but just remember that fleece is a bit stretchier than cotton and felt, so be careful not to pull on it when you're cutting and sewing.

LEATHER

If you're lucky enough to be allowed to use an old piece of leather, be extra careful and maybe even use a thimble while you're stitching. Leather is really thick and needles don't like to go through it very easily.

STUFFING

You'll need to stuff most of these super-cute makes to add the cuddly and squishable factor. There are loads of different stuffing materials you can use.

Try these ideas:

Cotton or polyester filling

This is the traditional stuffing and can be bought at a range of shops. If you get a high-quality filler, you'll get a professional-looking make. No lumps or anything!

Dried beans

This is another popular choice and gives a different feel. This is good for juggling balls, door stops and makes where you want a beanie feel.

Dried rice

Here's another popular option, similar to dried beans. And you probably already have some at home! Just ask your parents if you can use it first.

Potpourri

See if you can track down some scented filling like dried lavender. A softie stuffed with a scented filling makes an awesome gift!

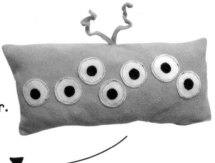

You can even try socks, wool, tissues or newspaper if you want to use what you've got lying around at home. This won't feel as professional as cotton filling, but it will make each softie unique!

When you stitch up the hole you've used to stuff your softie, try this trick to make the hole invisible:

Fold the fabric inside, tuck it in neatly and use tiny stitches to close the hole. The rough edges will be secretly hidden!

15

SOME STITCHES

Running stitch

Running stitch is the most basic of stitches. You simply bring your needle up through your fabric at point A and down again at point B to make a little line of thread. If you keep doing this in a straight line, going in and out of the fabric, you can sew a basic seam and stitch fabric together.

Backstitch

Backstitching is taking the running stitch to the next level. Start at point B, bringing your needle up through the fabric, and stitch back down through point A. Then bring your needle under the fabric, past point B, come up at point C and then down again at point D. Because you're going over the stitches, this is a super solid way to stitch two pieces of fabric together.

Satin stitch

Use the running stitch, but do a whole bunch side by side to make a shiny, satiny row of stitches.

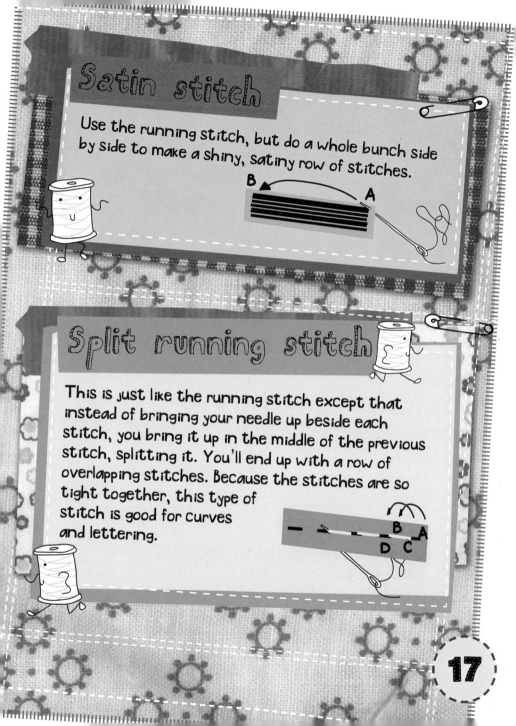

B ← A

Split running stitch

This is just like the running stitch except that instead of bringing your needle up beside each stitch, you bring it up in the middle of the previous stitch, splitting it. You'll end up with a row of overlapping stitches. Because the stitches are so tight together, this type of stitch is good for curves and lettering.

B A
D C

START TO STITCH

You're probably **thinking**, all this sounds so awesome and I can't wait to get started... but how DO I start?

- Firstly, get your needle and thread ready.
- Cut a piece of thread about an arm's length.
- Then thread your needle (get the thin little piece of thread through the tiny hole in the needle).

Have patience! You can do it!

- Once the thread is through the hole, move the needle to the middle of the thread and fold the thread in half. Having a double layer of thread will keep your stitches super strong.
- Lastly, tie the two ends together with a knot near the end of the thread. You may need to tie a few knots on top of each other so the thread doesn't slip through your fabric.

Finishing stitching

OK, so you know how to get started, but once you start, how do you stop? You can't just leave your needle hanging there! To finish up, do a few stitches on top of each other to secure the thread, or, if you want the end to look super tidy, stitch through the thread on the underside of the fabric a few times so no one will know the extra stitches are there but you.

When you're happy that your stitches aren't going anywhere, snip the thread close to the fabric – but not so close that it comes right out! **Then your needle is finally free.**

Wait, there's one more thing!

Sewing on a button!

1. Thread your needle with some thread that matches the colour of the button.

2. Lay the button in place on the material.

3. From under the material, push the needle through the fabric and up through one of the holes of the button.

4. Pull the thread all the way up, until the knot is tight against the fabric.

5. Next – you can probably guess! – is to go back down through another hole in the button, and straight down through the fabric.

6. Repeat this three more times to secure the button in place. If the button has four holes, do this three times diagonally one way, and three times diagonally in the other two holes.

7. When you've finished, make sure your needle is under the fabric. Thread it through the thread under the material and tie a double knot.

And that's it!

HOW TO APPLIQUÉ

What does appliqué mean, anyway? It's simple, really. We're cutting out shapes of one fabric and sticking them to another. This cushion is done this way.

We're going to use adhesive web to do the sticking.

love

I was done with appliqué.

One pretty important thing to remember is that your final picture is going to be a mirror image of the template you use. It gets flipped over, so if you're doing letters, remember to draw them backwards!

How to appliqué

1. Trace a pattern from a template at the back of the book, photocopy one of the templates or draw your own onto the paper side of the adhesive web.

2. Cut roughly around the edges of the shape. This is your chance to be messy – it doesn't have to be perfect yet!

3. Place the shape adhesive side down on the fabric you're using for the shape. Ask an adult to iron it in place. If you're using patterned material, make sure you stick the paper to the non-patterned side.

Fabric

4. No more Mr Messy Guy! Cut carefully around the edges of your shape. This time you're cutting the paper and the fabric since they are stuck together.

Template

5. Peel the backing paper off the shape and turn it over. The side with the adhesive on it will be rough, and the other side will be untouched, so you'll know which is which if you get confused.

6. Place the shape on a cushion, quilt or some other softie. Ask an adult to iron it in place with a cool iron. Press the iron down instead of sliding it on the material so the shape doesn't move around.

7. Lift the iron and check out your awesome appliqué. Ta-da! That shape should be stuck on good!

COLOUR PALETTES

Changing the colours you use for your makes can totally change the feel of your whole outfit. Mix up your colours to go from geek chic to girlie girl or sporty to rock. Choose materials in the colours in these palettes to get your style just right!

Pick your palette

Girlie girl

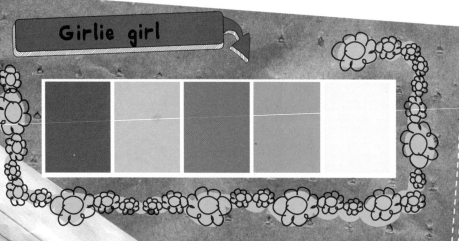

Sporty style

Geek chic

Rock chick

23

Let's Get Making

SOCK SOFTIES

HELLO

27

SOCK MONSTER

To make this scary (but still super-cute) monster,
YOU'LL NEED:

- 1 old sock (washed, please!)
- 1 small piece of felt, cut to the shape of a tooth (the felt that comes with this book works well!)
- 1 large button
- 1 covered button (wrap material around the button and fasten with glue or stitches at the back)
- Black ribbon, about 13cm long
- Black cotton thread
- Stuffing

HERE'S WHAT YOU DO:

1. Cut your sock across at the heel so you're only working with the flat foot bit.

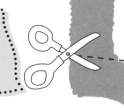

2. To give your monster eyes, stitch the two buttons to the sock.

3. To give your monster a mouth, use the running stitch to attach the ribbon to the sock.

GLUE

4. Glue on the tooth.

5. Fill your monster with the stuffing, making him as chubby or skinny as you like.

6. Stitch up the opening of the sock so none of the monster's insides come oozing out.

AAARRGHH! I AM THE SOCK MONSTER!

SOCK RABBIT

Step up your sock makes by taking them to the next level — this sock rabbit combines a sock with felt for an even more professional feel.

To make this super-cute rabbit, YOU'LL NEED:

- 1 sock
- 2 buttons
- Black cotton thread
- 1 circle of felt, 5.5cm across
- 2 pieces of fabric, cut to the shape of bunny ears
- Stuffing

HERE'S WHAT YOU DO:

1. Cut off the top (from the heel up) and bottom (from the toes down) of the sock.

Top

2. Fit the circle of felt into the opening at the bottom of the sock, with the felt overlapping the sock by about 5mm.

Bottom

3. Using the backstitch, sew all the way around the circle to attach the felt to the sock and close the bottom hole.

Felt

30

4. To give your bunny eyes, stitch the buttons to the sock.

5. To give your bunny a nose, stitch diagonally across several times.

6. Stuff your rabbit with cotton stuffing, beans or even tissues.

7. Pin the ears in place at the top of the rabbit, placing the ends just slightly inside the opening at the top of the sock.

8. Stitch across the opening using the backstitch to close the hole and attach the ears all in one go.

31

FUN WITH FELT

Felt is such an easy material to use, and it makes seriously soft characters. Try the teddy or dolls on the next pages, or try your own ideas. Felt works in any shape and size!

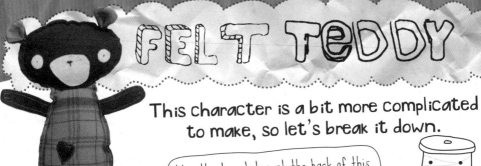

FELT TEDDY

This character is a bit more complicated to make, so let's break it down.

Use the templates at the back of this book to get just the right bear shape!

To make the HEAD AND EARS, YOU'LL NEED:

- 2 circles of white felt for eyes
- 1 piece of white felt for the mouth
- 2 large pieces of brown felt, cut to the shape of a teddy head
- 2 pieces of patterned fabric, cut to the shape of ears
- 2 pieces of brown felt, cut to the shape of ears
- Black cotton thread
- Stuffing

MAKE THE EARS FIRST:

 1. Place one piece of the patterned fabric and one piece of the brown ear felt back to back (pattern facing in).

 2. Stitch all the way around the ear, leaving a small hole at the bottom.

 34

 3. Use the little hole to turn the ear right side out.

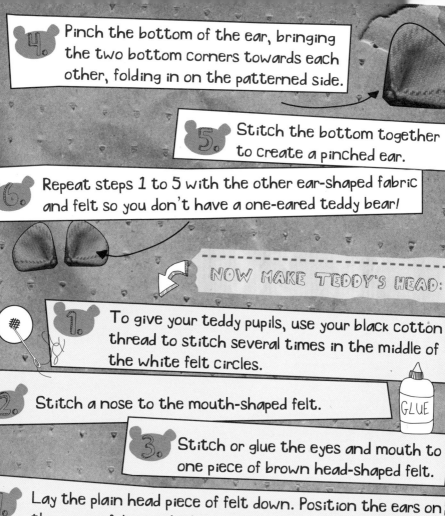

4. Pinch the bottom of the ear, bringing the two bottom corners towards each other, folding in on the patterned side.

5. Stitch the bottom together to create a pinched ear.

6. Repeat steps 1 to 5 with the other ear-shaped fabric and felt so you don't have a one-eared teddy bear!

NOW MAKE TEDDY'S HEAD:

1. To give your teddy pupils, use your black cotton thread to stitch several times in the middle of the white felt circles.

2. Stitch a nose to the mouth-shaped felt.

GLUE

3. Stitch or glue the eyes and mouth to one piece of brown head-shaped felt.

4. Lay the plain head piece of felt down. Position the ears on this piece, fabric side down. Then place the face piece of felt face down against the plain felt. Your ears should be between the pieces of felt.

5. Stitch around the face, attaching the front and back and making sure the ears are secured as you go. Leave a small hole at the bottom.

Make continues on next page

6. Turn the head the right side out and stuff the head with your stuffing.

To give your teddy a body, YOU'LL NEED:

- Patterned fabric (use the same as for the ears) cut to the shape of a bear body
- 4 felt strips, about 2cm x 6.5cm (for the arms and legs)
- 1 large brown piece of felt, cut to the shape of the bear's body
- Brown cotton thread
- Stuffing

NOW MAKE TEDDY'S BODY:

 1. Lay the brown felt body down and place the fabric pattern side down on top of it.

 2. Position the arms and legs in place, just in between the fabric and felt.

 3. Start stitching at the bottom and work your way around the body, stopping a little before where you started to leave a small hole.

4. Turn the body right side out and stuff the body with stuffing.

 36

Now stitch it all together!

TEDDY IN A TREE

37

FELT DOLLY

To make a little dolly, use the exact same steps as for the teddy on pages 34 to 37, but use different colours of felt and different facial features to make this softie girlie rather than furry! Add stuffed arms and legs, too!

Attach the hair and clothes after you've put your doll together.

38

GIRLS JUST WANNA HAVE FUN!

39

MINI ME

Mini me dolls are seriously cute. It's you, but mini! Again, make a doll using the same steps as you did for the teddy on pages 34 to 37. But this time, pick materials that match the real you!

If your hair is brown and straight, pick brown felt and cut it into the shape of your own 'do. If your hair is black and curly, how about using wool or pipe cleaners instead? This is your chance to be creative!

Choose fabrics that match your own style when dressing your doll, too.

Then carry her with you everywhere. People will think they're seeing double!

A mini me of your friends makes an awesome gift!

Double Trouble

41

MINI MASCOTS

Use the techniques on the previous pages to make yourself a teeny tiny softie. Make him out of felt or socks or whatever material you like best – the only difference from the earlier makes is that he's mini!

Very small but very CUTE

Be creative – go cute, quirky or COOL!

Take your mini mascot with you everywhere for good luck - and for fun!

He likes to hang off tote bags...

and hang out in the park...

careful he doesn't get lost out there!

Use one of the templates at the back of this book or draw your own character to cut out.

43

PATCHWORK MASTERPIECES

Patchwork is patch-tastic fun! This is your chance to piece together random bits of material that you've already got. To create a super-stylin' softie, try choosing materials that all come from one of the colour palettes on pages 22 and 23.

PATCHWORK POLLY, OWL DIVA

This owl works really well in any size — teeny tiny or extra large. Use the template at the back of the book. Try different colours to change Diva Polly to Casual Patchwork Pete, or whatever type of owl you fancy!

YOU'LL NEED:

- 2 pieces of fabric, cut to an owl shape
- 2 white felt circles
- 2 coloured felt circles, slightly larger than the white felt ones
- 2 buttons
- 1 semi-circle of coloured felt
- 1 brown felt triangle
- 2 pieces of felt, cut to the shape of wings
- White cotton thread

HERE'S WHAT YOU DO:

1. Stitch or glue the circles of coloured felt to one piece of owl body fabric.

2. Stitch or glue the white circles on top of the coloured circles. GLUE

3. Stitch the buttons in the middle of the circles.

46

4. Stitch or glue the semi-circle to the bottom of the owl body to give your owl a belly.

5. Glue the brown felt triangle beak in place.

Body fabric

6. Place the owl face down on top of the other owl body fabric. Position the wing ends between the two pieces of fabric and stitch all around the body, securing the wings in place as you go. Leave a small hole.

Owl face down

7. Turn the owl right side out and stuff Polly (or Pete...) with stuffing.

8. Stitch up the small hole using the overlock stitch.

Mirror, mirror on the wall... Looking good, dah-ling!

PATCHWORK CHARLIE CHICK

This is another little guy who can stay small or be blown up nice and big.

YOU'LL NEED:

- 2 pieces of white felt, cut to a chick shape
- 1 piece of red felt, cut to the shape of hair
- 2 pieces of red felt, cut to the shape of feet
- 1 piece of orange felt, cut to the shape of a beak
- Patterned fabric, about 5.5cm x 10cm
- Stuffing
- Black and white cotton thread

HERE'S WHAT YOU DO:

1. Stitch eyes to one piece of the white felt using the black cotton thread and a split stitch.

2. Stitch or glue the beak to the face.

3. Stitch the patterned fabric to the bottom half of the chick body front using the running stitch.

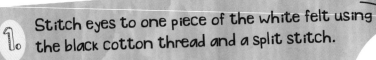

4. Place the chick face down on top of the second piece of felt chick body.

48

5. Pop the feet and hair in place between the two pieces of fabric.

6. Stitch all the way around, securing the feet and hair as you go and leaving a small hole at the side of the chick.

7. Turn the chick the right way out.

8. Stuff your chicklet with stuffing and stitch up the hole.

Chick face down

2nd piece of chick felt body

And here's Charlie!

PATCHWORK BiLLY BUNNY

Use the same instructions as for Charlie Chick to make this patchwork bunny, but just make sure to replace the beak with a little mouth and the hair with some big bunny ears!

PATCHWORK PALS GO

EXPLORING

51

5-A-DAY

How many times have you been told you need to eat your 5-a-day? Give in for once, and make the cutest fruit and veg ever to have 5-a-day every day!

Pear

Mushroom

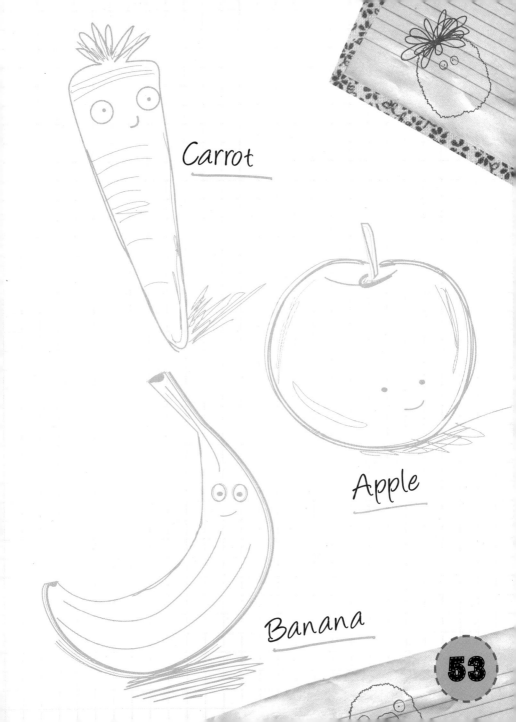

Carrot

Apple

Banana

53

KENNETH CARROT

Kenneth is the coolest and happiest carrot around. He is so excited that he'll be the number one of your 5-a-day!

YOU'LL NEED:

- 2 pieces of orange felt, cut to long triangles
- 1 small piece of green felt, snipped to look like a carrot top
- Orange and black cotton thread
- Stuffing

HERE'S WHAT YOU DO:

 To make Kenneth look very carroty, stitch a zigzag pattern on your orange felt pieces.

 On one of the pieces of orange felt, use a split running stitch to give Kenneth his eyes and mouth.

 Place the piece with Kenneth's eyes and mouth face down on the second piece of orange felt.

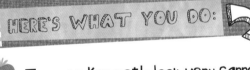

4. Position the carrot top between the orange felt pieces and stitch all the way around, securing the carrot top as you go and leaving a small gap in Kenneth's side.

5. Turn Kenneth right side out and add the stuffing.

6. Stitch up the hole using the orange cotton thread.

Now you've got one of your 5-a-day!

LOVE YOUR VEG.

Try making the other fruit and veg using the techniques you've learned in other makes!

CUDDLY CUSHIONS

Long, short, square or shaped, cushions are the ultimate cuddly make. They're a great touch to a sofa, armchair, bed or even the floor... Pile up lots of cushions in a corner for a snuggly little nook to read, write or just escape from your pesky little brother!

Make the cushions
on the next pages
and then try
to come up with
some designs of
your own!

SQUARE CUSHION COVER

This cushion is simple yet makes a serious splash on your sofa. First, find a plain cushion that needs a cover.

Tweet

YOU'LL NEED:

- ◎ 1 square piece of plain fabric, about 2cm longer on each side than your cushion
- ◎ 1 square piece of patterned fabric, the same size as the plain fabric square
- ◎ Fabric, buttons, felt, ribbons – anything to make your cushion stand out!
- ◎ Velcro, the length of one side of the plain fabric square
- ◎ Black and white cotton thread

HERE'S WHAT YOU DO:

1. Stitch, glue or appliqué your design onto the plain fabric square.

GLUE

2. Turn the design face down and stitch the Velcro piece along the bottom of the square.

Velcro strip

3. Turn the patterned fabric face down and stitch the other part of the Velcro along one edge.

4. Place the design face down against the patterned fabric square (pattern facing the design).

Make sure the Velcro pieces are lined up!

5. Stitch along the two sides and the top of the cushion using the backstitch, leaving the Velcro edges open.

6. Turn the cover right side out. Then pop the cushion in and keep it secure by sticking the Velcro together.

LONG ALIEN CUSHION

This extraterrestrial cushion will bring extraordinary attention to your sofa or bed!

YOU'LL NEED:

- 2 pieces of fabric, about 60cm x 30cm. Fleece works well!
- 7 white felt circles, for the eyes
- 7 small black felt circles, for the pupils
- 2 pieces of fabric or felt, 16cm x 4cm, for the antennae
- 2 pieces of thin wire, each 16cm long
- White and black cotton thread and glue
- Stuffing

TO MAKE THE EYES:

For a cool alien effect, do a running stitch around each white circle with black cotton thread, and then glue the black pupil to the middle of each eye.

TO MAKE THE ANTENNAE:

Fold one thin piece of fabric in half with the wire inside and stitch all the way around using a running stitch. Do the same for the other antenna.

Folded in half

Wire inside

TO MAKE THE CUSHION:

Put the two pieces of fabric together (outsides facing in), and stitch around the outside using the backstitch, leaving a small gap. Turn right side out and stuff, then sew up the small hole using the split running stitch.

Glue all seven eyes on. Sew the bottom of each antenna to the top of the cushion's back and then twist them for the final touch.

Hey human, I'm watching you!

61

CUTE CLOUD CUSHION

This cute white cloud brings no rain — only smiles!

YOU'LL NEED:

- 2 pieces of white fleece, cut to the shape of a cloud
- Black felt for the eyes and mouth
- White cotton thread
- Stuffing

HERE'S WHAT YOU DO:

1. Place the fabric pieces against each other, inside out. Stitch around the outside, leaving a small hole.

2. Turn right side out and stuff.

3. Stitch up the hole using white thread and the split running stitch.

4. Glue the eyes and mouth in place.

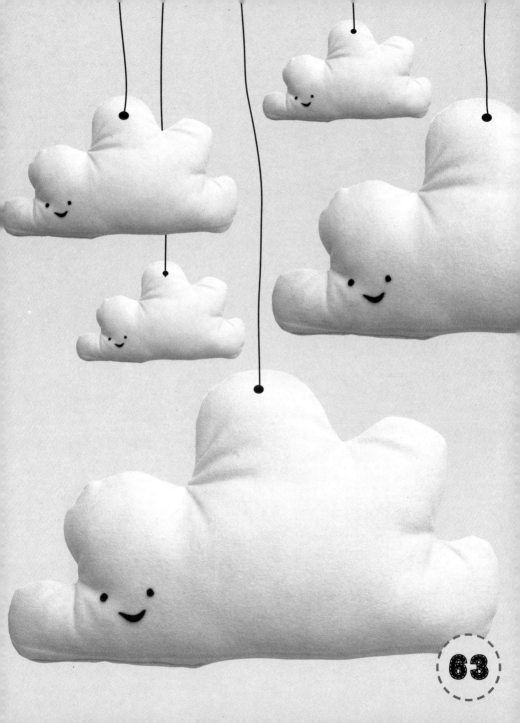

COSY EGG COSIES

Keep your boiled eggs cosy with these super-cute egg warmers.

- ▶ 2 pieces of black felt, about 9.5cm at the base
- ▶ 2 white felt circles
- ▶ 1 small triangle of orange felt for the beak
- ▶ 2 buttons
- ▶ Patterned fabric for his belly, about 6cm at the base
- ▶ 2 pieces of black felt for the wings
- ▶ White and black cotton thread and glue

HERE'S WHAT YOU DO:

 Stitch or glue the white felt circles to one piece of black felt, and stitch the buttons on.

 Glue on the beak.

 Glue or stitch on the patterned belly fabric.

4. Place the penguin face down on the other piece of black felt.

Base layer

Top layer

Wings in between

5. Place the wings between the fabric. Stitch around the penguin sides and top, but don't touch the bottom.

6. Turn right side out.

Use the same process to make an edgy egg warmer. Try a badge and patterned fabric instead of felt and cute penguin features.

FUNKY FINGER PUPPETS

Finger puppets are fun gifts for friends and perfect for when you want to impress.

Make them using the same technique as for the egg cosies on pages 64 and 65, but fit the size to fingers instead of eggs. They'll probably be long and thin instead of short and stout.

Then go crazy with finger skits!

Businessman

Schoolgirl

Super-cute puppet show!

Rabbit

JUGGLING CHICKENS

Whether you're talented in the juggling department or not, impress your audience with these seriously silly juggling chickens.

1. Find some cool patterned fabric and cut out six squares.

Hair

2. For each set, just like you've done for other makes, place the fabric together, pattern facing in. Place the beak and hair between the squares.

Pattern facing in

Beak

3. Stitch around the edges, securing the beak and hair as you go and leaving a small hole.

Use the super-secure backstitch so your chicks are ready for serious juggling action.

4. Turn right side out. Fill the juggling balls about 2/3 full with beans, lentils or rice.

5. Stitch up the holes carefully so no filling can slip out. Glue some eyes in place.

GLUE

Juggle!

Psst, you're facing the wrong way!

FLOWER POWER

Do you get tired of flowers wilting? Well, here you go: a flower that will never die! Vary the fabric, shapes and size to make a quirky bouquet to brighten up your room or to brighten up someone's day!

YOU'LL NEED:

- 2 pieces of patterned fabric, cut to the shape of a flower
- 1 large button
- 2 pieces of green felt, cut to the shape of leaves
- white cotton thread
- 1 green pencil
- Stuffing

and glue

If you don't have a green pencil, just paint one!

HERE'S WHAT YOU DO:

 Place the flower pieces together, pattern facing in. Stitch the pieces together around the edges, leaving a small hole. Turn right side out.

 Stuff with stuffing and stitch up the hole.

 Stitch the button to the centre of the flower.

Stitch around each leaf to add realistic leaf-like detail.

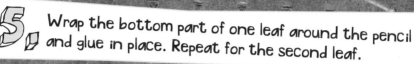 Wrap the bottom part of one leaf around the pencil and glue in place. Repeat for the second leaf.

Glue the flower to the top part of the pencil. Make sure to press in place well so the flower doesn't fall off!

Show off your flower in an old jug. Put some sticky tack at the bottom of the jug and push the pencil in so your flower stands up straight.

SWEET DREAMS eye MASKS

Do you or someone you know need a good night's sleep? Try out this super-sweet eye mask for sweet dreams and peaceful nights.

YOU'LL NEED:

☆ 1 piece of patterned fabric, cut to the shape of an eye mask
☆ 1 piece of soft fabric, also eye-mask shaped (this needs to be super soft - an old fleece jumper works well)
☆ 1 piece of thick fabric, also eye-mask shaped, to be used as the middle padding
☆ 2 pieces of ribbon, each about 30cm long
☆ Felt or buttons to decorate
☆ Cotton thread

HERE'S WHAT YOU DO:

1. First, decorate the patterned fabric. This Night Night mask has words stitched on felt using a split running stitch, but you could try out buttons or ribbon or other felt shapes to adorn the mask with loveliness, too.

Try out quirky patterns too. How about a face on a face?

74

2. Next, lay the soft fabric on a table, soft side down. Then put the thick fabric on top of that and the patterned fabric on top of that, pattern facing up.

Patterned fabric   Thick fabric   Soft fabric

3. Position the ribbons on either side of the mask, with the ends tucked in the layers of fabric.

4. Stitch all the way around using the backstitch.

And that's it! A dark and good night's sleep is yours! Night night!

night

night

SWEET DREAMS...

COMFY QUILTS

Quilts are super-impressive makes if you can pull them off. Give them away as awesome gifts — or just keep them yourself for a cold, rainy day! They look seriously smart across your bed, too.

- ◎ 1 piece of square fabric — this is for the main part of the quilt and can be as big as you like!
- ◎ 1 smaller piece of fabric to give a patchwork feel
- ◎ 1 piece of fabric, about 2cm smaller on all sides than the front quilt piece
- ◎ 5 pieces of shaped fabric — try the robot template at the back of the book or any other pattern that suits your style
- ◎ Thick fleece or wadding (a thick material useful for stuffing quilts), 2cm smaller on all sides than the front quilt piece
- ◎ White cotton thread

Although sewing around a big quilt by hand works just fine, it can take ages... This is a good time to ask an adult to help you get started on a sewing machine!

HERE'S WHAT YOU DO:

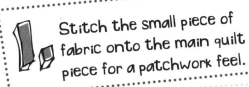 Stitch the small piece of fabric onto the main quilt piece for a patchwork feel.

 Stitch, glue or appliqué your design onto the front of the quilt.

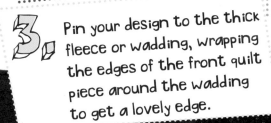 Pin your design to the thick fleece or wadding, wrapping the edges of the front quilt piece around the wadding to get a lovely edge.

 Pin the second piece of fabric to the back.

 Stitch all the way around the quilt using the backstitch. Or ask an adult to help you with a sewing machine!

Snug as a bug in a... quilt

79

BUILD A BLANKET

Try piecing more pieces of fabric together for a real patchwork feel for your quilt...

Or go with different PATTERNS and SHAPES to change up the style.

Instead of a decorative quilt, try a snuggly blanket made of fleece. If you haven't got an old fleece shirt as big as a blanket, you can buy a metre of fleece at a fabric shop for a low price. Fabric shops usually have plenty of different patterns to choose from, too.

When you've got your fleece, stitch shapes to it, or simply snip into one end, making 5cm cuts in every 2cm to get a fringed effect.

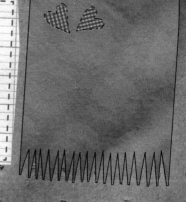

If you want a gift that leaves a lasting impression, a fleece like this is your ticket. It's simple and inexpensive, but such a thoughtful present.

POM-POM FUN

Pom-poms are adorable little mates.

YOU'LL NEED:

2 pieces of cardboard
Wool - and lots of it!
Decorative felt and ribbon

HERE'S WHAT YOU DO:

1. Use a compass to draw a circle about 5cm across on the cardboard, and cut out. From the centre of the circle, draw another smaller circle, 2cm across, and cut this out. Repeat to make one more ring.

2. Put the two pieces of cardboard together to get one sturdy donut.

3. Wind the wool around the donut. Work your way around until all the card is well covered.

4. Ask an adult to help you cut all the way around the outer edge of the donut, snipping the wool as you go.

5. Slide a piece of wool between the two pieces of cardboard and wrap it around the donut. Pull tight to tie all the pieces of yarn together. Then remove the cardboard.

82

6. Fluff up the pom-pom and trim it to make it nice and neat. Glue on the eyes and ribbon!

DOOR SIGN

Does your room keep getting invaded by nosy mothers and pesky siblings? If your voice isn't loud enough, try out this stylish sign instead.

YOU'LL NEED:

- Thin cardboard – cut out to the door sign template
- A bright-coloured piece of fabric, about 1cm larger all the way around than the door sign template
- A square piece of white felt, 8cm x 8cm
- Orange and white felt for the monster
- Yellow felt for the corners
- Black and white cotton thread and glue

HERE'S WHAT YOU DO:

1. Draw a line of glue all the way around the edges of the cardboard. Wrap the bright fabric around, pressing the edges firmly against the back.

2. When the glue is dry, stitch around the edges (right through the cardboard) for a polished feel.

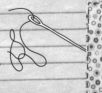

3. Stitch or use a permanent marker to write 'Keep Out' on the white felt, then stitch or glue the felt to the door sign.

4. Stitch or glue the yellow felt corners onto the cardboard.

5. Stitch or glue the eyes and tooth onto the orange monster and then glue or stitch him onto the sign.

Hang on your door and watch this monster work his **MAGIC!**

KEEP OUT!

BOOK COVER

We're not supposed to judge a book by its cover, but we can still make the cover look as good as possible!

HERE'S WHAT YOU DO:

1. First, wrap a piece of paper around the book as if you're wrapping a present very neatly. This will show you where the folds need to go and how to cut the corners.

Paper

2. Place the paper on top of the fabric. Cut the fabric around the paper.

3. Fold the fabric around the book and pin the folds down. Ask an adult to iron the folds to keep them stiff.

4. Stitch around the edges but leave the pockets on each side open so you can slip the front and back covers of the book inside.

Pretty
easy
and
pretty
cool!

87

ALPHABET CUTENESS

You can spell anything you like in super-cute letters.
Let your imagination run wild!

YOU'LL NEED:

Fun fabric
White cotton thread
Stuffing

DO ONE LETTER AT A TIME:

1. Draw the letter on a piece of paper to make yourself a template. Cut out the paper letter and trace it onto the fabric.

2. Cut out the fabric letter.

3. Flip the template over to make the back of the letter – trace and cut again.

4. Place the fabric letters together, pattern facing in. Stitch all the way around, leaving a small gap.

5. Turn the fabric the right side out and stuff.

6. Tuck the rough edges inside and stitch up the hole.

7. Repeat the steps for each letter!

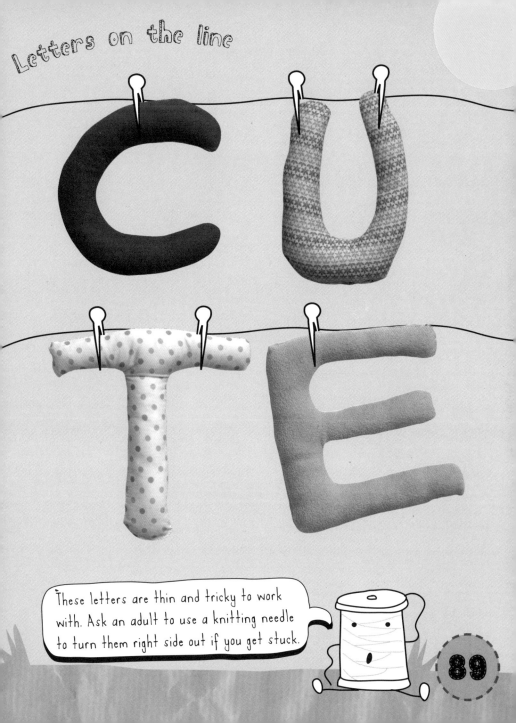

These letters are thin and tricky to work with. Ask an adult to use a knitting needle to turn them right side out if you get stuck.

MOLLY MUG

Molly Mug is a happy little mug who likes to hang out with other teacups. Make sure you give her a nice big smile!

YOU'LL NEED:

- 1 cardboard circle, 7cm across
- 1 cardboard circle, 6cm across
- 1 brown felt circle, 8cm across
- 1 blue felt circle, 7cm across
- 1 piece of blue felt, 20cm x 8cm
- 1 piece of blue felt, 9cm x 5cm (for the handle)
- Blue cotton thread and glue
- Black felt for the eyes and mouth
- Stuffing

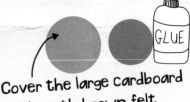

HERE'S WHAT YOU DO:

1. Cover the large cardboard circle with brown felt and the smaller circle with blue felt: wrap the felt around the cardboard and glue the edges down underneath.

2. Fold the large piece of felt in half and stitch the short edges together to get a ring.

3. Stitch along the long edge, pleating the fabric as you go along so it puckers. Pull the thread tightly to close the bottom hole. This gives you your teacup shape.

4. Glue the blue felt circle to the bottom of the cup, under all the puckers. Stitch around the edge to keep this secure.

5. Stuff the cup with stuffing.

6. Place the brown felt circle on top of the mug and stitch it to the mug top edge.

7. To make the handle, fold the fabric in half lengthways and stitch along three edges. Stuff and then sew up the hole. Stitch the handle ends to the mug.

8. Glue on Molly's eyes and smile.

Tea time!

SIMON SEPTOPUS

An octopus has eight legs, and a septopus has seven.
Simon is a silly little septopus!

Flip back to page 14 if you want a reminder about different types of stuffing!

YOU'LL NEED:

- 1 circle of flannel, 14cm across
- 7 legs of flannel, 4cm x 9cm
- Stuffing
- Black felt for the eyes and mouth
- Cotton thread to match your flannel

HERE'S WHAT YOU DO:

1. Place the stuffing in the middle of the flannel circle

2. Grab all the flannel around the stuffing and bring it up to meet above the stuffing so you have a stuffed flannel ball.

3. Stitch around the fabric to secure it in place and so no stuffing shows through.

Stuffing

4. For each leg, fold the flannel strip in half and stitch along the top and two sides. Stuff with stuffing and stitch to the bottom of the stuffed flannel ball.

Stuffing

5. Stick the eyes and mouth in place to give Simon his personality.

Simon says... make!

93

TINY TOADSTOOL PINCUSHION

Have you ever seen such an adorable place to keep your pins?
Super cute!

YOU'LL NEED:

White felt, 3cm x 16cm

1 circle of cardboard, 5cm across

1 circle of red felt, 9cm across

Small round dots of white felt

Black thread, stuffing, glue

HERE'S WHAT YOU DO:

 Starting at a short edge, roll the white felt into a cylinder. Draw on the eyes and mouth.

 Unroll the felt and stitch the face on with black thread.

 Now roll the felt up again and glue the end in place.

Place the red felt flat on a table. Pop a bit of stuffing in the middle and then place the cardboard on top.

Cardboard

Stuffing

Red Felt

 Do a loose running stitch around the edge of the red felt circle, pulling as you go so the middle gap is being closed over the stuffing and cardboard.

 When you're done there should be a small hole under the cap of the toadstool. Wedge the white roll just inside this and glue in place.

Glue the white dots to the top of the toadstool.

Allow to dry then pin away!

CREDITS

Crafts designed and made by Kate Woods

Photography by Mike Cooper and Darren Sawyer. Photo page 41 courtesy of iStockphoto.

Illustrations by Caroline Martin and Clare Phillips

Words by Laura Baker and Kate Woods

Check out the other book in this series, I MADE IT MYSELF, for cool stuff to make and wear!